MW01122671

U.S. ARMED FORCES

U.S.
COAST
GUARD

By Jenny Mason

Kaleidoscope
Minneapolis, MN

BIGFOOT BOOKS

The Quest for Discovery Never Ends

This edition first published in 2024 by Kaleidoscope
Publishing, Inc.

No part of this publication may be reproduced in whole or in
part without written permission of the publisher.

For information regarding permission, write to
Kaleidoscope Publishing, Inc.
6012 Blue Circle Drive
Minnetonka, MN 55343

Library of Congress Control Number
2023937057

ISBN
978-1-64519-738-6 (library bound)
978-1-64519-786-7 (ebook)

Text copyright © 2024 by Kaleidoscope Publishing, Inc.
All-Star Sports, Bigfoot Books, and associated logos are
trademarks and/or registered trademarks of Kaleidoscope
Publishing, Inc.

Printed in the United States of America.

FIND ME IF YOU CAN!

Bigfoot lurks within
one of the images in
this book. It's up to
you to find him!

TABLE OF
CONTENTS

Chapter 1

ALWAYS READY

Winds slam the ocean. Waves curl and break. A US Coast Guard **vessel** cuts through the dangerous waters. Its crew searches for a lost sailboat. The Coast Guard is an armed military force. Armed forces defend the nation. The Coast Guard is also like the police. It enforces the law and it saves lives. It must protect the US coast, major rivers, and the Great Lakes. It monitors all ports and harbors. The Coast Guard also operates around the world. Crews help other forces on missions.

Special missions take the Coast Guard around the world. Crews bust ocean ice sheets. They clean pollution and respond to natural disasters. They stop illegal **migrants**. No wonder their motto is "Always Ready."

FUN FACT

The Coast Guard patrols 95,000 miles (153,000 km) of coastline and 15,000 miles (24,100 km) of rivers.

US ARMED FORCES
BRANCHES

 Air Force

 Marine Corps

 Army

 Navy

 Coast Guard

 Space Force

A crewmember spots the sailboat. It has flipped over, or **capsized**. Survivors cling to the sinking vessel. The Coast Guard crew dart to the rescue.

What we call the Coast Guard today began as the Cutter Service in the 1790s. That year, Congress ordered 10 cutter ships to be built. Those ships protected American goods at sea. They broke up pirate gangs. They also rescued sinking ships.

The government created the official Coast Guard in 1915. Back then, they managed **lighthouses** and inspected steamships. The new service was called the US Coast Guard. They are also nicknamed Coasties.

The survivors are pulled onto the Coast Guard boat. Their injuries are treated. The crew helping them is **diverse**.

Men and women serve in the Coast Guard. People from all backgrounds serve. This has been the case for nearly 200 years. Women served as official lighthouse keepers. African Americans worked for the Life-Saving Service. Diverse students joined the academy to become officers in the 1950s. At the time, only white, male students were allowed at military academies.

FIRSTS

Captain Michael Healy was the first African American cutter commander. He operated the polar ship *Bear* (1887–1895). Florence Finch was the first Asian American woman to serve in the Coast Guard. She served during World War II. In 1991, the first Hispanic women directed Coastie ships and aircraft: Katherine Tiongson sailed; Marilyn Melendez Dykman flew. In 2006, Vivien Crea took over the second-highest rank. She was the first woman to do so in any military branch.

COAST GUARD RANK

COMMANDANT: top official

VICE ADMIRALS: one commands the Atlantic while another controls the Pacific

REAR ADMIRALS: control shorelines—land, sea, and air space

OFFICERS: include Captain, Commander, and Lieutenant; officers command the vessels, aircraft, and crews

JUNIOR OFFICERS: include Chief Warrant Officer, Petty Officer, and Seaman

Vice Admiral Vivien Crea

Captain Michael Healy

Florence Finch

9

UNITED STATES COAST GUARD
TIMELINE

1789
US Lighthouse Service
established. ▼

1776
American colonies
win independence
from England.

▲
1834
Steamboat Inspection
Service created.

1775   1825

1800   1850

1788
The US Constitution
is ratified.

1790
Alexander Hamilton
proposes a Revenue
Cutter Service. ▼

1884
Bureau of Navigation opens.

1915
US Coast Guard created to combine all sea-related services, except the Navy.

1875

1900

1925

1878
US Life-Saving Service begins operations.

Chapter 2

FLOAT, FLY, AND BARK

A speedboat darts across the sea. It is loaded with dangerous chemicals. A Coast Guard cutter chases the boat. Coasties use many different ships, boats, and aircraft. Ships are large. Some are longer than 400 feet (122 m). That is more than the length of two space shuttles. **Buoy** tenders are smaller ships. Cutters are fast patrol ships.

Boats are shorter than 65 feet (20 m). Lifeboats and response boats are the most commonly used vessels.

FUN FACT

The Coast Guard is developing a new fleet of robotic ships called Tritons. They will sail without crews on board.

USCG motor lifeboats

Coast Guard Cutter Polar Star

The Cutter Vigorous carries out law enforcement and rescue missions.

627

626   U.S. COAST GUARD

White and blue waves crash against a rocky cliff. A hiker stumbles. He falls onto a ledge. His leg is broken. Witnesses call 9-1-1. Soon a Coast Guard helicopter arrives. The hiker is rescued. Helicopters are important Coast Guard equipment. The Jayhawk helicopter can travel 600 miles (966 km). It can carry away six survivors from an accident. It flies at speeds greater than 200 miles per hour (322 km/h).

The Coast Guard also uses planes for different missions. The C-27 plane is powerful. It can cover more than 2,600 miles (4,200 km). Its **wingspan** is longer than a line of three school buses!

ICEBREAKERS

The Coast Guard uses icebreaker ships. They sail through icy polar regions. They bust up thick ice sheets. Icebreakers help cruise ships. They deliver supplies to Arctic villages. They take science equipment to Antarctica. Research stations there use this gear. They gather weather data. This helps the weather service.

Cables creak as cranes lift shipping containers off ships. The metal boxes stack like colorful toy blocks. A Coast Guard team watches the busy **port**. Eleven million containers come to the United States each year. They deliver the goods we buy. Some hide illegal drugs. Toxic substances. Kidnapped people. Stolen goods. Containers hide these items, too. The Coast Guard team must inspect the containers.

They use a special tool: dogs! Dogs have powerful noses. They can smell dangerous chemicals. These dogs sniff and snuff. Their tails wag. *Bark! Bark! Bark!* Here is something! Coast Guard dogs also inspect ships out at sea.

Ricky, the Coastie dog, wears a hoisting vest, goggles, and ear covers. This way, he can be lowered from helicopters to help with missions.

Chapter 3

SHIP-SHAPE

"One! Two! Three! Four!" Coast Guard recruits count their push-ups. They are outside before sunrise. This is basic training. The Coast Guard is a small military branch. They currently have 40,400 active-duty service members.

The US Coast Guard is one of the toughest forces to join. There are different ways to join the Coast Guard. An adult can enlist for duty and work for the Coast Guard full-time. Reservists train to be Coasties. But they serve only when there is a **crisis**. Other people join the officer academy. They train to be leaders in the Coast Guard.

People with a shellfish allergy are not eligible to join the US Coast Guard.

The recruits run laps as the Sun rises. Basic training has many fitness tests. Run 1.5 miles (2.4 km) in 12.5 minutes. Complete 29 push-ups in 60 seconds. Swim 320 feet (98 m) in 5 minutes.

Recruits take many classes. They learn about first aid and using weapons. When basic training ends, recruits become ensigns. They learn to sail or fly. Later, ensigns choose a special job. Some will repair boats and aircraft. Some become expert sailors. Welding. Cooking. Fighting floods. There are hundreds of choices.

UNIFORMS

Uniforms are important in the armed forces. They create a team spirit. They also communicate rank. A uniform helps identify who is in charge in an emergency. Coast Guard uniforms come in different colors like winter blue, tropical blue, white, and khaki.

FUN FACT

Ensigns with musical talent can join the Coast Guard band.

Lightning flashes. The hurricane batters the Gulf of Mexico. Victims are drowning. A Coast Guard helicopter appears. A crewmember drops from the aircraft. *Splash!* She is a rescue swimmer, or Aviation Survival Technician (AST). The helicopter lowers a rescue basket. The rescue swimmer lifts one man into the basket. He is pulled to safety. The rescue swimmer rushes to the next victim. ASTs pluck people and pets off cliffs and rooftops. Their training is the toughest of all armed forces programs. About 73 percent of AST recruits quit.

A SECRET SKILL

All 350 rescue swimmers have a secret skill. Can you guess what it is?

A. Swim 25 yards (23 m) under water.

B. Tow a victim the length of two football fields.

C. Provide emergency medical treatments.

D. Sew.

ASTs can do all these things! Sewing is their secret skill. They repair their own parachutes. They mend their flight suits. They sew their own gear bags. They even make their own name tags!

Chapter 4

IN WAR AND PEACE

September 11, 2001. Dark smoke swallows New York City. Terrorists crashed two planes into skyscrapers. The United States is under attack. All armed forces go on high alert. The Coast Guard patrols the coastlines. They will stop any more threats coming by sea.

When the United States must go to war, the Coast Guard always helps. Cutters fought British ships in the War of 1812. They stopped enemy ships from reaching US ports in World War I (1914–1918). During World War II, they battled German submarines from 1941 to 1945. The Korean War. The Vietnam War. The US wars with Afghanistan and Iraq. The list of battles is long. Coasties fight bravely. Some even die. To serve is to **sacrifice**.

241,000 men and women Coasties served in World War II.

Ukrainian soldiers surround the Boatswain's Mate (BM). More soldiers cover the deck. Their icy blue and gray fatigues look like the dark ocean. No, this Coast Guard ship has not been captured. It is a gift. Russia attacked Ukraine in 2014 and 2022. The United States promised to help Ukraine. The Coast Guard **donated** several ships. This crew will teach the soldiers how to sail them.

FUN FACT

The United States gifted 18 fast patrol boats to Ukraine in 2022.

A Coast Guard boat chases a pod of whales. One whale is caught in fishing nets. The Coasties must slow down the whale. They tie a heavy **anchor** to his tail. They cut away the nets. They release the whale. He swims away with the pod.

The Coast Guard is busy even when the United States is not at war. Coasties work on all seven continents. They help poorer nations create new coast guards.

FISH POLICE

Fish are a major food source around the world. About 40 percent of all people would go hungry without fish to eat. Fishing laws help all people share this resource. Criminal fishing ignores these laws. It harms the environment. Catches are not limited. Fish populations shrink. Local fishers cannot feed their communities. Other animals that eat fish also go hungry. The Coast Guard prevents illegal fishing. They play an important role in keeping the world fed.

EVERY DAY, THE COAST GUARD:
- Saves 12 lives
- Responds to 60 distress calls
- Runs 44 search and rescue missions
- Completes 107 inspections
- Makes 48 patrols on water
- Screens 329 vessels for threats
- Investigates 34 pollution events
- Repairs 80 buoys and other navigation aids

Coasties are busy during peacetime. They must protect ocean environments. They respond to oil spills. They stop polluters. They lead rescues and clean up after hurricanes. More than 5,000 Coasties responded to Hurricanes Katrina and Rita in 2005. An earthquake destroyed Haiti in 2010. The Coast Guard arrived to help. At home. Far away. On the water. In the air. For the US Coast Guard, every day is a chance to serve.

BEYOND THE BOOK

After reading the book, it's time to think about what you learned. Try the following exercises to jump-start your ideas.

THINK

GO ON PATROL. Where might you go to learn more about the US Coast Guard? Has someone you know served as a Coastie? What questions would you ask them? Keep in mind that wars leave behind painful memories. Service members might prefer to tell you about their training or fellow crewmembers. Are there any sailing museums in your area?

CREATE

SALUTE. Imagine you have been asked to design a new Coast Guard ship! Grab some color pencils and paper. Sketch your idea. How big would your ship be? What would you name it? What colors would you paint it? Where would it sail?

SHARE

GIVE THANKS. Write a letter to a veteran. That is someone who has served in the military. Share what you have learned about the US Armed Forces. How have you benefited from their service? How would your life be different without the armed forces and their missions?

GROW

SHAPE UP. Are you fit enough to serve in the Coast Guard? How many sit-ups or push-ups can you do? How far can you run or swim? Maybe your body works differently. What are ways you can exercise? Why do you think Coastie recruits have to exercise so much? Why is fitness important?

RESEARCH NINJA

Visit *www.ninjaresearcher.com/7386* to learn how
to take your research skills and book report writing to the next level!

Research

DIGITAL
LITERACY
TOOLS

SEARCH LIKE A PRO
Learn how to use search engines to find useful websites.

FACT OR FAKE
Discover how you can tell a trusted website from an untrustworthy resource.

TEXT DETECTIVE
Explore how to zero in on the information you need most.

SHOW YOUR WORK
Research responsibly—learn how to cite sources.

Write

DOWNLOADABLE
BOOK REPORT
FORMS

GET TO THE POINT
Learn how to express your main ideas.

PLAN OF ATTACK
Learn prewriting exercises and create an outline.

Further Resources

BOOKS

Brink, Tracy Vonder. *The United States Coast Guard*. Mankato, MN: Capstone Pebble Books, 2021.

Morey, Allan. *U.S. Armed Forces: U.S. Coast Guard*. Minneapolis, MN: Jump! Inc., 2020.

Tougias, Michael J. and Casey Sherman. *True Rescue: The Finest Hours: The True Story of a Heroic Sea Rescue*. New York: Henry Holt, 2021.

WEBSITES

FACTSURFER

Factsurfer.com gives you a safe, fun way to find more information.

1. Go to www.factsurfer.com.

2. Enter "Coast Guard" into the search box and click 🔍

3. Select your book cover to see a list of related websites.

Glossary

anchor: A heavy metal object that is lowered from a ship or boat to keep it from drifting

buoy: A floating marker, often with a bell or a light, that shows boats where to go or warns them of underwater dangers

capsize: To turn over in the water

crisis: A time of severe difficulty or danger

diverse: Having many different types or kinds

donate: To give something to a charity or cause

lighthouse: A tower set in or near the sea with a flashing light at the top that helps ships avoid danger

migrants: People who move from one place to another, especially to find work or escape wars

patrol: To walk or travel around an area to protect it or the people within it

port: A harbor or place where boats and ships can dock or anchor safely

sacrifice: To give up something you value or enjoy for the sake of something that is more important

vessel: A ship or large boat

wingspan: The distance between the ends of the wings on birds or aircraft

About the Author

Jenny Mason is a story-hunter. She explores foreign countries, canyon mazes, and burial crypts to gather the facts that make the best true tales. She received an MFA in Writing for Children and Young Adults from the Vermont College of Fine Arts. She also holds an MPhil from Trinity College Dublin. You will often find her swimming in murky lakes. But alas, she will never qualify for the Coast Guard. She is allergic to shellfish.

Index

PHOTO CREDITS